CELTIC FOLKSONGS

FOR ALL AGES

JAMES CURNOW
TIMOTHY CAMPBELL

CURNOW
MUSIC

Order Number: CMP 1034-05-400

James Curnow, Timothy Campbell
Celtic Folksongs for all ages
F / E♭ Horn

CD Accompaniment tracks created by James L. Hosay

CD number: 19-063-3 CMP
ISBN 90-431-2294-7

CELTIC FOLK SONGS FOR ALL AGES

INTRODUCTION

This book is a sampling of rich tunes and ballads specifically distinctive to the cultures of Scotland, Newfoundland and Ireland. Initially associated with everyday rural activities, these memorable melodies have been married with colorful accompaniments to offer a variety of musical settings for all performers.

The accompaniment CD (included in the solo book) provides all musicians the opportunity to perform for organized gatherings or spontaneous productions among friends and relatives. There are two tracks for each tune. The first track includes a sample performance of the solo with the accompaniment. The second track is just the accompaniment, allowing the soloist to play along. There is also a separate Piano accompaniment available. So, delight in the richness of "CELTIC FOLK SONGS FOR ALL AGES" and continue the spirit with which folk music has been passed down through cultures near and far.

INSTRUMENTATION GUIDE

C Instrument (CMP 1031-05)	-	Piccolo, Flute, Oboe, or any Mallet Percussion instrument.
Bb Instrument (CMP 1032-05)	-	Bb Clarinet, Bb Bass Clarinet, Bb Cornet, Bb Trumpet, Bb Flugel Horn, Bb Tenor Saxophone, Bb Trombone T.C., Bb Euphonium/Baritone T.C., Bb Tuba T.C.
Eb Instrument (CMP 1033-05)	-	Eb Alto Clarinet, Eb Alto Saxophone, Eb Baritone Saxophone, Eb Tuba T.C.
F/Eb Instrument (CMP 1034-05)	-	F/Eb Horn
Bass Clef Instrument (CMP 1035-05)	-	Cello, Double Bass, Bassoon, Trombone B.C., Euphonium/Baritone B.C., Tuba B.C.

Piano Accompaniment (CMP 1036-05)

JAMES CURNOW

James Curnow was born in Port Huron, Michigan and raised in Royal Oak, Michigan. He lives in Nicholasville, Kentucky where he is president, composer, and educational consultant for Curnow Music Press, Inc. of Wilmore, Kentucky, publishers of significant music for concert band and brass band. He also serves as Composer-in-residence (Emeritus) on the faculty of Asbury College in Wilmore, Kentucky, and is editor of all music publications for The Salvation Army in Atlanta, Georgia.

His formal training was received at Wayne State University (Detroit, Michigan) and at Michigan State University (East Lansing, Michigan), where he was a euphonium student of Leonard Falcone, and a conducting student of Dr. Harry Begian. His studies in composition and arranging were with F. Maxwell Wood, James Gibb, Jere Hutchinson, and Irwin Fischer.

James Curnow has taught in all areas of instrumental music, both in the public schools (five years), and on the college and university level (twenty-six years). He is a member of several professional organizations, including the American Bandmasters Association, College Band Directors National Association and Wind Ensembles and the American Society of Composers, Authors and Publishers (ASCAP). In 1980 he received the National Band Association's Citation of Excellence. In 1985, while a tenured Associate Professor at the University of Illinois, Champaign-Urbana, Mr. Curnow was honored as an outstanding faculty member. Among his most recent honors are inclusion in Who's Who in America, Who's Who in the South and Southwest, and Composer of the Year (1997) by the Kentucky Music Teachers Association and the National Music Teachers Association. He has received annual ASCAP standard awards since 1979.

As a conductor, composer and clinician, Curnow has traveled throughout the United States, Canada, Australia, Japan and Europe where his music has received wide acclaim. He has won several awards for band compositions including the ASBDA/Volkwein Composition Award in 1977 (*Symphonic Triptych*) and 1979 (*Collage for Band*), the ABA/Ostwald Award in 1980 (*Mutanza*) and 1984 (Symphonic Variants for Euphonium and Band), the 1985 Sixth International Competition of Original Compositions for Band (*Australian Variants Suite*), and the 1994 Coup de Vents Composition Competition of Le Havre, France (*Lochinvar*).

Curnow has been commissioned to write over two hundred works for concert band, brass band, orchestra, choir and various vocal and instrumental ensembles. His published works now number well over four hundred. His most recent commissions include the Tokyo Symphony Orchestra (*Symphonic Variants for Euphonium and Orchestra*), the United States Army Band (Pershing's Own, Washington, D.C.-Lochinvar, Symphonic Poem for Winds and Percussion), Roger Behrend and the DEG Music Products, Inc. and Willson Band Instrument Companies (*Concerto for Euphonium and Orchestra*), the Olympic Fanfare and Theme for the Olympic Flag (Atlanta Committee for the Olympic Games, 1996), the Kentucky Music Teachers Association/National Music Teachers Association in 1997 (*On Poems of John Keats for String Quartet*) and Michigan State University Bands (John Whitwell, Director of Bands) in honor of David Catron's twenty-six years of service to the university and the university bands (*Ode And Epinicion*).

TIMOTHY CAMPBELL

Timothy Campbell was born in Guelph, Ontario, Canada. He currently lives in Manchester, Connecticut where he teaches K – 12 instrumental and choral music for Cornerstone Christian School. He is also the personnel manager and contractor for the Summer Music Festival orchestra in New London, Connecticut, where he has worked with such artists as Jane Glover, Robert Levin, Larry Rachleff, Norman Krieger, Donald Pippen, and Johnny Mathis.

He received his undergraduate degree from Asbury College in theory and composition. While attending Asbury he studied with James Curnow and garnered such accolades as the Kentucky Music Educators Composition Award and the Penniston Honors Competition awards for piano and composition. Under a full scholarship, he went on to the University of Connecticut where he completed his master's degree in music theory.

TABLE OF CONTENTS

Tracks with solo part and accompaniment

Tracks with accompaniment only

AIKEN DRUM

Scottish Folk Song
Arr. Timothy Campbell (ASCAP)

BELIEVE ME, IF ALL THOSE ENDEARING YOUNG CHARMS

Irish Folk Song
Arr. Timothy Campbell (ASCAP)

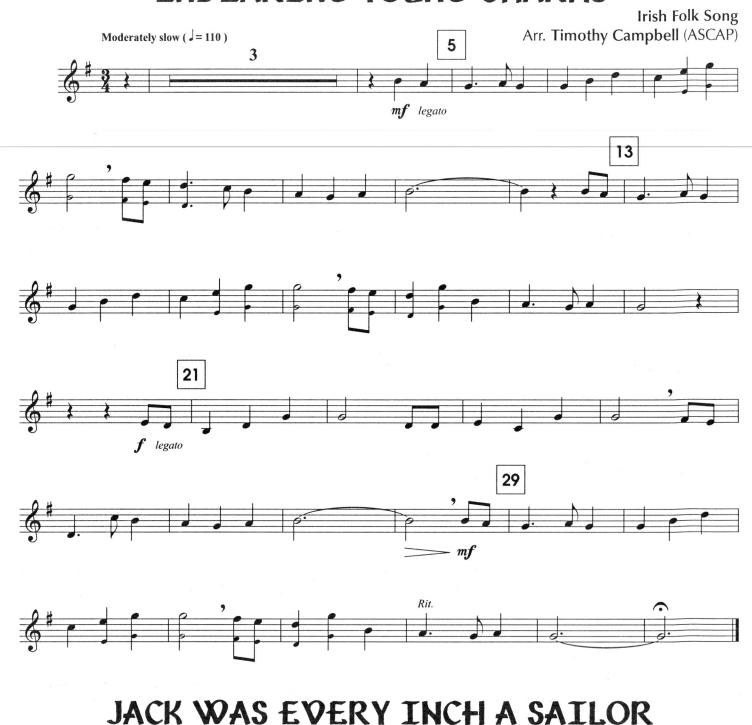

JACK WAS EVERY INCH A SAILOR

Newfoundland Folk Song
Arr. James Curnow (ASCAP)

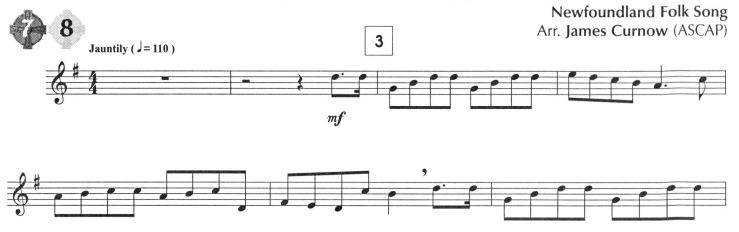

8   Copyright © 2005 by Curnow Music Press, Inc.

THE ASH GROVE

Welsh Folk Song
Arr. Timothy Campbell (ASCAP)

I'LL TELL ME MA

Irish Folk Song
Arr. Timothy Campbell (ASCAP)

THE BLUEBELLS OF SCOTLAND

Scottish Folk Song
Arr. James Curnow (ASCAP)

I'S THE B'Y

Newfoundland Folk Song
Arr. Timothy Campbell (ASCAP)

CMP 1034-05 F Horn

LOCH LOMOND

Scottish Folk Song
Arr. Timothy Campbell (ASCAP)

Copyright © 2005 by **Curnow Music Press, Inc.**

TOO-RA-LOO-RA-LOO-RAL

(That's An Irish Lullaby)

Irish Folk Song
Arr. **Timothy Campbell** (ASCAP)

CMP 1034-05 F Horn

LUKEY'S BOAT

Newfoundland Folk Song
Arr. Timothy Campbell (ASCAP)

WHEN IRISH EYES ARE SMILING

Irish Folk Song
Arr. Timothy Campbell (ASCAP)

CMP 1034-05 F Horn

Copyright © 2005 by **Curnow Music Press, Inc.**

MRS. MURPHY'S CHOWDER

Irish Folk Song
Arr. Timothy Campbell (ASCAP)

MOUNTAINS OF MOURNE

Irish Folk Song
Arr. Timothy Campbell (ASCAP)

THE IRISH WASHERWOMAN

Irish Folk Song
Arr. Timothy Campbell (ASCAP)

MOLLY MALONE

Newfoundland Folk Song
Arr. **Timothy Campbell** (ASCAP)

WE'LL RANT AND WE'LL ROAR

Newfoundland Folk Song
Arr. Timothy Campbell (ASCAP)

AIKEN DRUM

Scottish Folk Song
Arr. Timothy Campbell (ASCAP)

BELIEVE ME, IF ALL THOSE ENDEARING YOUNG CHARMS

Irish Folk Song
Arr. Timothy Campbell (ASCAP)

JACK WAS EVERY INCH A SAILOR

Newfoundland FolkSong
Arr. James Curnow (ASCAP)

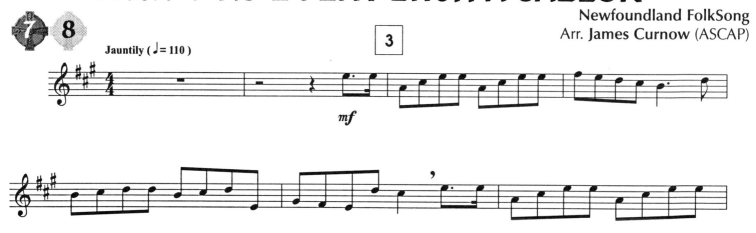

THE ASH GROVE

Welsh Folk Song
Arr. Timothy Campbell (ASCAP)

I'LL TELL ME MA

Irish Folk Song
Arr. Timothy Campbell (ASCAP)

THE BLUEBELLS OF SCOTLAND

Scottish Folk Song
Arr. James Curnow (ASCAP)

I'S THE B'Y

Newfoundland Folk Song
Arr. Timothy Campbell (ASCAP)

Copyright © 2005 by **Curnow Music Press, Inc.**

LOCH LOMOND

Scottish Folk Song
Arr. Timothy Campbell (ASCAP)

Copyright © 2005 by **Curnow Music Press, Inc.**

TOO-RA-LOO-RA-LOO-RAL

(That's An Irish Lullaby)

Irish Folk Song
Arr. Timothy Campbell (ASCAP)

LUKEY'S BOAT

Newfoundland Folk Song
Arr. Timothy Campbell (ASCAP)

WHEN IRISH EYES ARE SMILING

Irish Folk Song
Arr. Timothy Campbell (ASCAP)

MRS. MURPHY'S CHOWDER

Irish Folk Song
Arr. Timothy Campbell (ASCAP)

MOUNTAINS OF MOURNE

Irish Folk Song
Arr. Timothy Campbell (ASCAP)

THE IRISH WASHERWOMAN

Irish Folk Song
Arr. Timothy Campbell (ASCAP)

Copyright © 2005 by **Curnow Music Press, Inc.**

MOLLY MALONE

Newfoundland Folk Song
Arr. Timothy Campbell (ASCAP)

WE'LL RANT AND WE'LL ROAR

Newfoundland Folk Song
Arr. Timothy Campbell (ASCAP)

SUNDAY SCHOOL CLASSICS

These new arrangements of standard Sunday School songs provide the opportunity to play in many different styles, and to grow musically while performing in your church, or at other performance opportunities.

These arrangements are designed so that they can be used in two different ways, either as solos or as duets. Any combination of instruments can perform together. An accompaniment book is available if you want to use a live accompanist. If an accompanist is not available, you can use the enclosed CD accompaniment.

Available books:

C Instruments   (CMP 0658.02)
   (Piccolo, Flute, Oboe, or any Mallet Percussion instrument)

B♭ Instruments   (CMP 0659.02)
   (B♭ Clarinet, B♭ Tenor Saxophone, B♭ Trumpet, Euphonium T.C. and others)

E♭ Instruments   (CMP 0660.02)
   (E♭ Alto Saxophone, E♭ Baritone Saxophone and others)

F Horn or E♭ Horn   (CMP 0661.02)

B.C. Instruments   (CMP 0662.02)
   (Bassoon, Trombone, Euphonium and others)

Piano Accompaniment   (CMP 0663.02)

CAMPFIRE CLASSICS

Campfire Classics is a collection of timeless campfire classic folk songs. They are delightfully arranged in fresh settings by two of the foremost arrangers in the instrumental field. These arrangements are designed to be used in two different ways, either as a solo or as a duet. Any combination of instruments can perform together. As long as each performer has the appropriate book for the key of their instrument, any combination of instruments will work.

The accompaniment CD (included in the solo book) provides two tracks for each tune. The first track includes the accompaniment with the duet part (for accompanying a soloist). The second track includes the accompaniment only (for accompanying a duet).

Contents:
Bingo / Kum Ba Yah / A Little R & R / The Itsy Bitsy Spider / She'll Be Comin' 'Round The Mountain / There's a Hole in my Bucket / Row, Row, Row Your Boat / Hush, Little Baby, Don't You Cry / Study War No More / Just Plant a Watermelon

Available books:

C Instrument	(Piccolo, Flute, Oboe, or any Mallet Percussion instrument)	(CMP 0934.04)
B♭ Instruments	(B♭ Clarinet, B♭ Tenor Saxophone, B♭ Trumpet, Euphonium T.C. and others)	(CMP 0935.04)
E♭ Instruments	(E♭ Alto Saxophone, E♭ Baritone Saxophone and others)	(CMP 0936.04)
F Horn or E♭ Horn		(CMP 0937.04)
B.C. Instruments	(Bassoon, Trombone, Euphonium and others)	(CMP 0938.04)
Piano Accompaniment		(CMP 0939.04)